BURY AS IT WAS

Helen Barrett A.L.A.

Cover pictures: The Lancashire Fusiliers South African War memorial was unveiled in the Market Place on Saturday, 18th March, 1905. The memorial was the work of George Frampton, R.A., who was later famous for his statue of Peter Pan in Kensington Gardens, London. The figure is rather unusual in that many war memorials depict the soldier with his head bent in grief for his dead comrades, whereas Frampton decided to show the soldier's thirst for the battle and the will to carry on.

The bronze memorial was unveiled by Lord Derby, wearing his Lord Lieutenant's uniform, and the Mayor, Alderman Butcher, in accepting the memorial promised to preserve it and keep it in good condition.

At the close of the proceedings the troops paraded to the Drill Hall and the Co-op Hall for refreshments, and an old folks treat was later held in the Drill Hall, to mark the occasion. The Mayor attended, and seated next to him can be seen Bury's youngest ever Mayoress—Alderman Butcher's nine-year old daughter.

Published by Hendon Publishing Company Limited, Hendon Mill, Nelson, Lancashire.
Text © Helen Barrett, 1976
Printed by: Fretwell & Brian Ltd., Howden Hall, Silsden, Keighley, Yorks.

£1.40

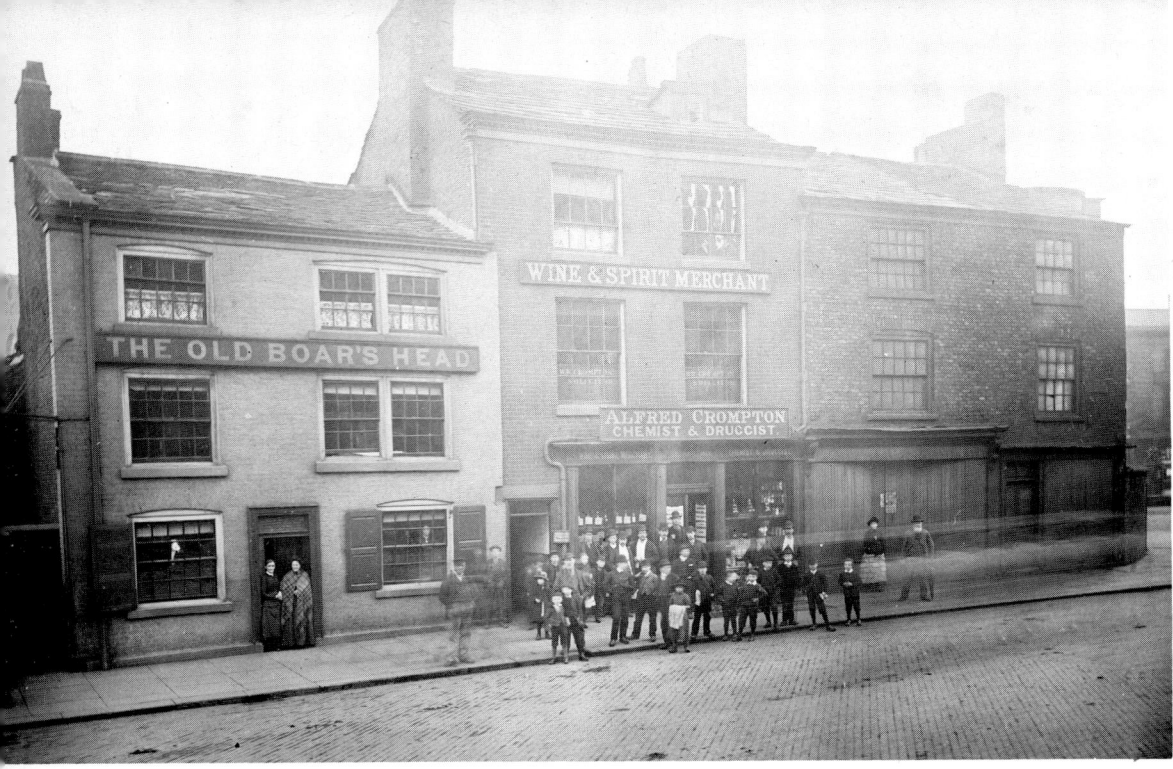

At the turn of the century a walk along 'The Rock' as we now know it would have taken us along four streets — Fleet Street, Rock Street, Stanley Street and Water Street. The four different names caused confusion and in 1935 the name 'The Rock' was officially adopted.

These two photographs show 'before and after' shots of Fleet Street. Fleet Street ran from the Parish Church to the junction with Union Street, and the top photograph is of the property opposite the Parish Church. Alfred Crompton, the chemist at number 4, was an ancestor of Richmal Crompton, the famous Bury born author of the 'William' books. Richmal—the daughter of the Rev. E. J. S. Lamburn, a master at Bury Grammar School—died in 1969, and Alfred Crompton in 1898.

The bottom photograph, dated about 1889 shows the Derby Chambers—next to Cromptons the Chemist—in the course of erection.

At the time the photograph was taken, work was in progress with the re-laying of the tramway. Steam trams had run along Fleet Street since 1886 and their enormous weight resulted in the track having to be relaid.

Shown on the right of the photograph are the premises of Giles Hewart, draper, the father of Gordon Hewart who in 1912 was to become Lord Chief Justice of England. Gordon was educated at Bury Grammar School from 1879 to 1884 and was called to the Bar in 1902. His first brief was from Bury Town Clerks Office—the case being held at Salford Hundred Sessions. Having taken silk in 1912 he became a K.C. and in 1916 Gordon became Solicitor-General. In 1940 he was created Viscount Hewart of Bury and he died in May 1943.

The cabman's shelter on the corner of Crompton Street and Fleet Street can be clearly seen and to the left the 'Hand and Shears' Inn, demolished in 1961.

Rock Street in 1910, and the site of the Hornby Buildings. The demolition of this property began in April 1933 but it was to be a complicated process, as many of the businesses in these premises were to be transferred to the new buildings. As the old buildings overlapped the new building line, it was decided to cut the old in half, so that the front portion could still be occupied. Meanwhile the rear portion was removed to afford sufficient space to allow the erection of the new premises.

Fleet Street was one of the main shopping areas of the town and situated on the corner of Union Street and Fleet Street was Downhams—a household name for over a century in the Bury district. Originally Henry Peel had an ironmonger's shop on this site and in January 1853, the twenty-two year old Joseph Downham took over the business. Robert Hall joined him in 1855 and a short time later Henry Turner came into the business. As trade increased more room was needed, and this handsome accommodation on the right of the photograph was erected in 1891. As well as these premises Downhams also had a spacious warehouse for agricultural implements and stabling for their horses at the Corn Market on Haymarket Street.

In 1969 Downham's linked-up with John Kay and Sons (Bury) Ltd., and the Fleet Street premises were demolished in March 1971.

Incidentally, Joseph Downham's father, a cabinet maker also named Joseph, was the first person to be buried in the Non-Conformist portion of Bury Cemetery after it was officially 'opened' in May 1869.

Queen Victoria's Diamond Jubilee in 1897 provided Bury people with an excuse for celebrating and decorating the town. The Fire Brigade were naturally anxious to do their bit, and provided this spectacle with their extending ladders. The model fire engine is still preserved in the Bury Museum and the photograph is taken looking towards Water Street.

At this time the Fire Brigade had a steam fire engine pulled by horses.

Only fairly recently have these shops and cottages on Chapel Row and Stanley Street been demolished. Seen on the left of the photograph is the gatepost of St. Johns church, which was demolished in 1967.

As German troops invaded Belgium in 1914, Arthur Ashworth, the founder of the Ashworth Chemical Works at Fernhill, launched an appeal in August, for clothing and bedding to help the distressed Belgians and the refugees. Bury people responded and in September 1914 this first load of clothing weighing 15 cwts, was sent from Bury to the Belgian Relief Fund. Mr. Ashworth paid for the sacks to be sent to the Belgian Consul in London, and then appealed again to the people of Bury for more clothing, and especially for socks and stockings.

At the same time, Belgian refugees began arriving at Hollymount Convent, Tottington.

Bury is justly proud of its associations with the Lancashire Fusiliers and the Militia Barracks and the Wellington Barracks housed companies of soldiers for many years.

Gallipoli Day is still commemorated in April each year and the Regiment's performance on that day in April 1915 when the 'Lancashire Landings' took place can be summed up in the words 'six V.C.s before breakfast'.

Lancashire Fusiliers Memorial, Wellington Barracks, dedicated to the Fusiliers who lost their lives in the Great War.

Left: As part of the 1911 Coronation festivities, an ox-roasting ceremony was held on the fairground.

Mrs. Albert Taylor, the wife of Councillor Taylor gave the ox which weighed 700 lbs. The ox was roasted on Wednesday, 7th July, over a charcoal fire, lit by the Mayor. Not being done over an open fire, perhaps the ox-roasting was not such a spectacular sight as one might imagine.

The roasting was completed by Thursday morning and Councillor Taylor and two of his employees cut the beef into portions, which were distributed to some 200 poor families, who also received a cabbage and a pot of dripping.

Councillor Taylor is the gentleman on the right of the photograph.

Top right: There can be few towns the same size as Bury who have benefitted as much as Bury has from the munificence of its citizens. Lord Derby, the main landowner was always generous and the Whitehead family of Haslam Hey were benefactors in no small way.

Approaching the town from Manchester Road, the Whitehead Clock Tower, built of beautiful Portland stone, (now stained with the copper deposits from the minerals used) has been a familiar landmark since 1914. The tower is built on the site of Belle Vue—once Dr. William Goodlad's private lunatic asylum—and it was the gift of Henry Whitehead, who wished to perpetuate the memory of his eminent brother, Dr. Walter Whitehead, a surgeon of world-wide repute.

Every stone came to the site numbered and ready to be placed in position, and the tower stands on a base of Aberdeen granite steps.

Walter was not the only famous member of the family—Robert Whitehead had invented the torpedo and the family were proud of their descent from John Kay, the inventor of the flying shuttle.

Behind the tower can be seen Duke Street, which linked Manchester Road and Knowsley Street. Duke Street was demolished in 1935 to make way for the Town Hall.

Bottom right: Silver Street in the tranquil days before the rush hour and the one-way system. The van in the centre belongs to Bury District Co-operative Society and immediately behind it is the old building of the Bury Trustee Savings Bank, demolished after the new building opened for business in 1966.

Top left: Manchester Road, Blackford Brow, was widened and improved during the 1930s. Public works of this nature were encouraged during this period so as to provide work for the unemployed, and a number of other roads in the Bury area were improved. The gentleman wearing the trilby hat is the foreman, Mr. F. Ward.

Bottom left: Although not one of Bury's oldest Non-Conformist churches, the architectural grandeur of Brunswick Methodist on North Street, certainly made it one of the most imposing.

Brunswick's beginnings dated back to the stormy days of the 1830s, when in 1836, "a schism rent asunder" the Sunday School of Union Street chapel. (Indeed a whole book could be written on the schisms in the Bury Non-Conformist churches of the eighteenth and nineteenth centuries!) It was customary for the Sunday School to meet in Clerke Street School and then at the appointed time to walk in procession to Union Street chapel for worship. But on one Sunday in 1836 the procession took a different route and whilst a few went to Union Street as usual, 176 teachers and 863 scholars marched to a warehouse in Paradise Street. This became known as —"The Tabernacle"— and the congregation worshipped there until the first Brunswick chapel opened in 1837.

The foundation stone of the first Brunswick chapel was laid on Whit-Friday 1836 and during the night not only was the stone removed, but also the articles which had been placed underneath. The first chapel became a school when the new church opened in December 1864.

Brunswick's 131 year history made an immense contribution to the spiritual and musical life of the town, and it was a matter of regret to many when it was demolished in 1968.

Right: And these handsome young men, sat upright and staring so solidly at the camera, were the members of the Bury Water Polo Team of 1896. The captain was Mr. S. Cheetham and the gentlemen on the back row are from the left: W. Jolly, McG. Beattie, C. E. Whitaker, and G. H. Studholme.

Very little has been discovered about the team, but perhaps patrons of the old Bury baths will remember a similar photograph hanging in the Baths office for many years. Mr. W. Nuttall, seated on the captain's right, was a swimming instructor who was tragically killed at Gallipoli in World War I.

Top left: Had local government not been reorganised in 1974, Bury would have celebrated its centenary as a borough in 1976. The town received its Charter of Incorporation in September 1876 and the first elections for thirty seats on the new council were held in November. The first meeting of the Bury Town Council took place on Thursday, 9th November and Alderman John Duckworth was chosen as the first Mayor. In 1888 Bury became a County Borough with the responsibility of providing more of its own municipal services. The Golden Jubilee Celebrations of 1926 were gay, exciting days and the children's pageant held on the Wellington Playing Field was an outstanding event. The 'Bury Times' described the pageant as 'a living representation of the Borough coat of arms'. Nearly 7,000 children took part and the display was directed by Mr. W. Morgan, a physical education instructor. The band of the 5th Battalion of the Lancashire Fusiliers played and fifteen special trams ran the children to the scene. The display was watched by parents and civic dignitaries and at the end of the display the Mayor, Councillor Hartley, rewarded the children by giving them an extra days holiday from school. To mark the jubilee, shopping festivals were held, a new playing field was opened, a special exhibition was held in the Art Gallery and an old folks treat was organised. At a special council meeting, Lord Derby was made a Freeman of the Borough.

Bottom left: The Municipal Offices and the Council Chamber occupied the upstairs of the Lancashire & Yorkshire Bank, (now Barclays) on Silver Street, and the rest of the corporation offices were scattered throughout the town centre.

The bank was built in 1867 for the Bury Banking Company, who on finding their premises in The Wylde too small, decided to erect a building "which should be an ornament to the town". Two features of the completed building were the fire-proof floors and the fine carvings in the exterior stone-work. In 1888 the Bury Banking Company amalgamated with the Lancashire and Yorkshire Bank, and in 1928 the name was changed to Martins Bank.

Right: The other side of Silver Street bedecked and garlanded in honour of the jubilee celebrations of 1926.

Although short in length Silver Street was one of the most attractively decorated streets in the town centre. The Conservative Club was festooned with flags and foliage and Webster & Peacocks, the grocers was tastefully decorated. On the left of the photograph can be seen one of the red and white pylons which were placed at various points in the town centre, and from which the floral garlands were suspended.

The Bury Guardian reported on September 11th that 'Bury has passed through a wonderful week. There has not been anything approaching the displays, the general decorations, or interest, in any event during the history of the Borough'.

A regular market has been held in Bury since the mid-fifteenth century when Henry VI granted Sir John Pilkington, the Lord of the Manor, a charter to hold a weekly market on Fridays. By the seventeenth century market day was Thursday and by 1826 a Saturday market was held.

Until 1839 the market was held in the Market Place, and the fishmongers laid out their fish on the fish stones —twelve curved stone blocks which occupied the site where Peel's statue now stands.

In December 1839, a new open market was erected on what is now Kay Gardens, and this was provided at Lord Derby's expense. Initially there was a poor response to the new market as the traders preferred their pitches in the Market Place, and so for some time the new building was used to house a company of foot soldiers. Finally, the traders did move in and the new market became as popular as the old. In November 1867 a glass and iron roof was fixed and structural alterations provided accommodation for more stalls.

In 1900 the roof was declared unsafe and the market closed to allow the roof to be removed. The town council had already decided that Lord Derby's market had "had its day" and in 1891 a competition was organised to select a suitable design for a new market.

The corner stone of the new building was laid in 1901, and the Mayor, John Battersby opened the market in December of the same year. That building remained virtually unaltered, apart from extensions, until the fire of November 1968 which gutted the building.

In 1947, Wednesday became a market day, and in 1953, Friday was added

Beginning with the upright photograph of H. Halstead, the grocer, then viewing clockwise, the photographs are of:
E. Derby, butcher, taken in 1926.
Lord Derby's market, on what is now Kay Gardens.
The old and the new markets.
Mary A. Cooper's tea and refreshment rooms.

Left: In marked contrast to the streamlined ambulance of today is this horse-drawn accident ambulance manufactured by Wilson and Stockall of Bury. Founded in 1877, the firm claimed to be the first patentees of ambulances. During the 1890s the company designed the Broughan carriage ambulance and became well-established as manufacturers of doctor's gigs. Hand ambulances were supplied to local authorities and police forces throughout the country and the firm were pioneers of motor ambulances.

The last ambulance to be made by Wilson and Stockall was purchased by Burnley Corporation in 1961.

Right: There must still be many 'Bobby Hall' looms in use all over the world, manufactured by Robert Hall & Sons of Hope Foundry, Bury. The firm enjoyed its heyday at the end of the Victorian era, and in 1906, trade being so good, this property was purchased so that the foundry could be extended. The firm had started in a two storey building with a ground floor space of only 72 square yards—but eventually the foundry occupied a five acre site on George Street and Spring Street.

Left: J. H. Parker's slipper works at Greenbrook Factory, Chesham and obviously a firm with plenty of work in its order books. Indeed, at the height of production the firm could turn out 24,000 pairs of slippers a week. J. H. Parker, a Rawtenstall councillor, started the Bury firm in 1905 with twenty people and the company was the first to make repairable sandals for children. Mr. Parker was a popular figure, well-known for his kindness and generosity to his employees and he was mourned by many after his untimely death in a road accident in August 1927.

Right: From 1880, children over the age of ten could be exempted from school to work part-time in factories, provided they had reached a certain educational standard. The age at which they could start work was gradually raised by successive Factory Acts and the raising of the school leaving age. The half-time system was finally abolished by the Education Act of 1918, by which all children were obliged to remain at school full-time until they reached the age of fourteen.

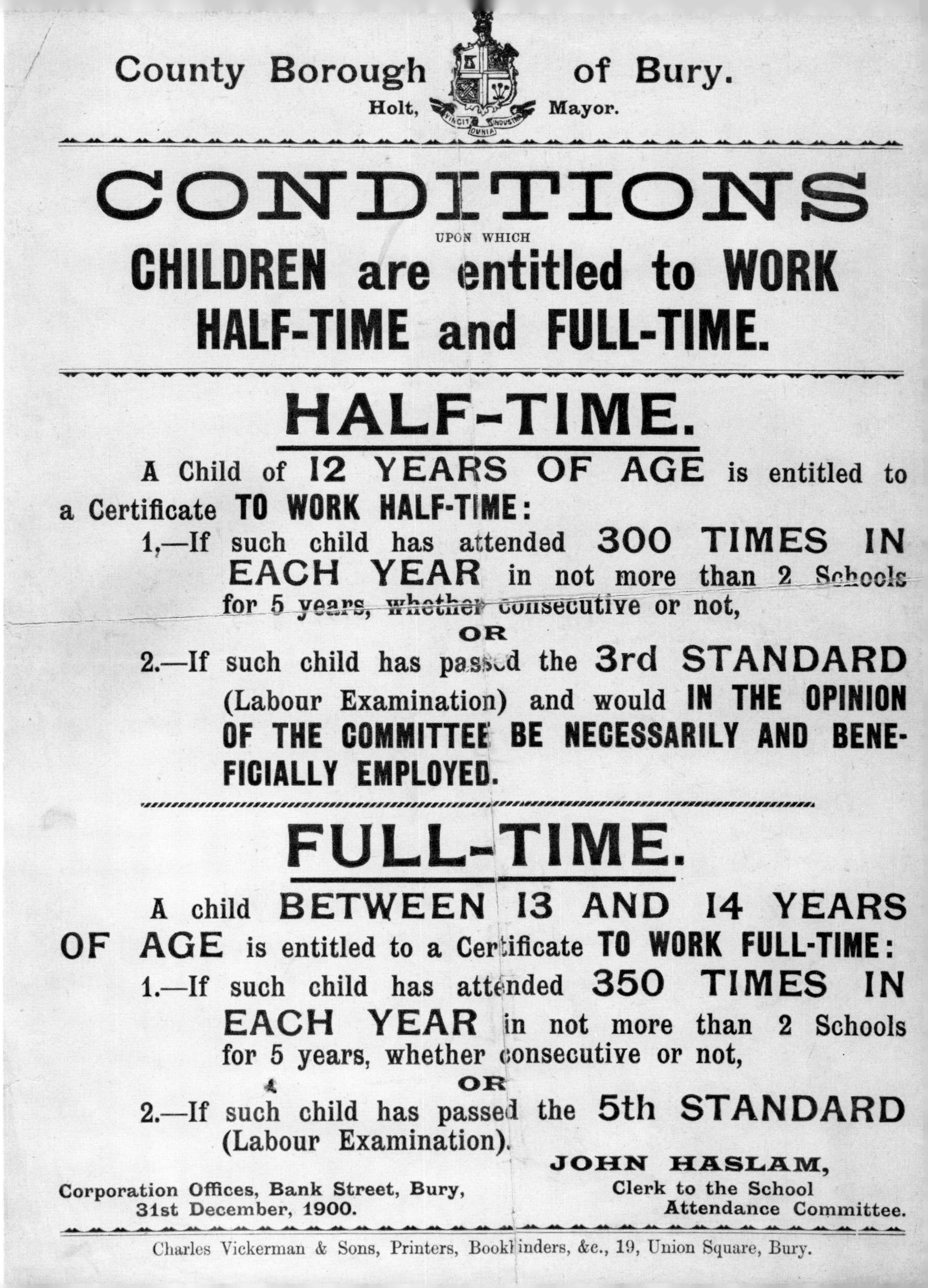

County Borough of Bury.
Holt, Mayor.

CONDITIONS
UPON WHICH
CHILDREN are entitled to WORK
HALF-TIME and FULL-TIME.

HALF-TIME.

A Child of 12 YEARS OF AGE is entitled to a Certificate TO WORK HALF-TIME:

1,—If such child has attended 300 TIMES IN EACH YEAR in not more than 2 Schools for 5 years, whether consecutive or not,

OR

2.—If such child has passed the 3rd STANDARD (Labour Examination) and would IN THE OPINION OF THE COMMITTEE BE NECESSARILY AND BENEFICIALLY EMPLOYED.

FULL-TIME.

A child BETWEEN 13 AND 14 YEARS OF AGE is entitled to a Certificate TO WORK FULL-TIME:

1.—If such child has attended 350 TIMES IN EACH YEAR in not more than 2 Schools for 5 years, whether consecutive or not,

OR

2.—If such child has passed the 5th STANDARD (Labour Examination).

JOHN HASLAM,
Clerk to the School
Attendance Committee.

Corporation Offices, Bank Street, Bury,
31st December, 1900.

Charles Vickerman & Sons, Printers, Bookbinders, &c., 19, Union Square, Bury.

Top left: Perhaps some former employees of Wormalds Timber Company will recognise themselves on this snapshot taken in 1913. Harold Chatterton is the man on the left on the front row and the young lad is Jimmy Haworth. Wormalds started in 1878 as an offshoot of an engineering firm established earlier. Mr. Wormald, the founder, began as a timber merchant in 1878 and on his death in 1914, the business was carried on by Harold Chatterton. In 1916 Sam Roberts, who was the financial partner sold out to Oliver Ashworth and Mr. Lemmon. Ultimately, Mr. Lemmon bought out Mr. Ashworth and Mr. Lemmon's son Harold carried on the business until its closure in 1973.

The firm specialised in home-grown timbers, particularly sycamores, and during the last war they supplied planks for the decks of landing craft.

Bottom left: From about 1870 until the Great War, the firm of John Slater, mineral water manufacturers, were well-known for their thirst quenching products. The works at Bedlam Green in 1871 and at Clay Bank, Rochdale Road made drinks with the most appetising names—gingerette, raspberry, aerated ginger beer, peppermint and cider, as well as botanic brews and cordials. It was essentially a family business and whilst John Slater, the founder of the business was dead by the time this photograph was taken, his widow Susan is shown in the centre of the picture. John's son John and his grandson John are seated on the cart on the left, and seated on the cart on the right is Fred Slater, son of Susan and immediately in front of him is Esther Slater, Susan's daughter-in-law and mother of John Slater III. The other lady is Sarah, Susan's daughter.

Left: A wet day for the Protestant Whit-Walk and a fine day for the Roman Catholic walk on Whit-Sunday. The photographs are undated but were obviously taken after the erection of the War Memorial (in 1924.) Evidence suggests that the photographs could well be of the 1932 walks. During the early 1920s, the Roman Catholics decided to walk on Whit-Sunday, and the procession passing the Derby Hotel shows the Guild of St. Agnes, associated with either St. Joseph's or the Guardian Angels' Church.

The custom of Whit-Walks dates back to the early nineteenth century when Manchester children assembled in St. Ann's Square to take part in a service. The Whit-Friday Walks were abandoned in the 1960s when Spring Bank Holiday replaced the Friday as a holiday.

Union Square and the crowds assembled for the hymn singing, during a Whit-walk. The square dated back to July 1784 when Richard Howarth, a printer laid the corner stone of the first building.

During May 1939, Bury began to make preparations in case war should break out. Union Square was excavated and air raid shelters made of reinforced concrete cast *in situ* were constructed beneath the Square. The shelters were 6' 7'' high, over 4 feet wide and could accommodate 700 people. By Whit-Friday the workmen had filled in the trenches and tidied up and the Sunday Schools were able to enjoy their hymn singing as usual.

The Square disappeared during the town centre redevelopment of the 1960s.

A reminder of the Theatre Royal will bring back happy memories for many Bury people. The work of James Byrom of Bury, the theatre opened with the pantomime 'Little Red Riding Hood' on 26th December 1889. The builders were busily trying to complete their work whilst the manager, Mr. Purcell was showing the Mayor and his civic party to their seats. Throughout the 1890s and into the 1900s the theatre enjoyed considerable success. Those were the days when 'House Full' notices were posted outside and when theatre-goers were packed in like sardines.

Names like George Elliot, Harry Tate, Ellen Terry and Sir Henry Irving made the theatre one of the most popular. Indeed, up to 1915, the theatre had the largest stage in the North, and it was on this stage in the days before the Great War that Charlie Chaplin appeared in some of the Fred Karno slapstick shows.

To the minds of many older people will spring the name of Otto C. Culling, the theatre's most famous manager. He made a colourful impression on the Bury theatre world at the beginning of this century, with his black cloak and silk top hat and he commanded respect from his employees and contemporaries. He took an active part in the life of the town, being for some years a councillor for Redvales ward. He and his wife Ada are buried in Bury Cemetary.

The last live show was presented in 1933 and the theatre became a cinema in 1933. For many years the Bury Athenaeum Amateur Operatic Society performed their annual show at the theatre—their last production being 'Princess Charming' in 1933.

Springside House, Walmersley, was built for the Rev. Sir William Henry Clerke, a former Rector of Bury, on the site of the farmhouse known as Gooseford. Sir William went into the Fleet Prison for debt about 1808 and his property was contracted for by William Yates. Mr. Yates lived at the Rectory for a time and then removed to Springside, where he died in 1813. Rector Clerke died in prison in 1818 and Springside was purchased by William Grant. Daniel Grant was living there in 1855 and the last occupant was Richard Olive who died in 1917. Springside was demolished in 1918.

A book on Bury would be incomplete without reference to its most famous son, Sir Robert Peel, the younger. Peel was born at Chamber Hall on 5th February 1788, and he was the eldest son of Robert Peel, formerly of Oswaldtwistle; and Ellen, daughter of William Yates, a partner in the firm of Haworth, Peel and Yates, cotton manufacturers of Bury.

Sir Robert Peel was educated by James Hargreaves, the curate of Bury Parish Church, but at the age of ten he and his family removed to Drayton Manor near Tamworth, Staffordshire.

It is said that on hearing of the birth of his eldest son, Sir Robert Peel's father fell on his knees, gave thanks to God and vowed that he would give his child to his country.

The front part of Chamber Hall dated from the eighteenth century whilst the rear portion was built in 1611. In 1867 the hall became a Baptist Theological College and in 1909 it was demolished to make way for the electricity works.

Peel's cradle and the nine inch thick dated stone from Chamber Hall can still be seen in the Bury Museum.

Top left: Bolton Street Station was opened in August 1847, although a passenger train service between Bury and Rawtenstall had been in operation since September 1846. Prior to the building of Bolton Street Station, passengers had to board the train from a small station situated behind the Lord Nelson Inn, and the line was reached via a steep slope.

The railway was administered by the East Lancashire Railway Company who had their headquarters in a large building on the east side of the station. The entrance to the headquarters was through two magnificent wrought-iron gates, each bearing the E.L.R. crest. When the gates were removed by British Rail during the modernisation work, one of the crests was mounted in the new booking hall of the station.

The London, Midland and Scottish Railway announced in March 1946 that the station would be modernised under a long-term rebuilding plan, but in May 1947 an early morning fire gutted the booking hall, approaches and the footbridge. The railways were nationalised in 1948 and British Railways were asked by the Bury Town Council to improve the station. Towards the end of 1950 the station was demolished and building work later began on the new station. An acute shortage of building materials delayed the work, but eventually the new station opened on 30th June 1952.

For many years trams were a part of the everyday street scene, but photographs of them still evoke a feeling of nostalgia in many of us.

After the horse buses came the steam trams operated by the Manchester, Bury, Rochdale and Oldham Steam

Tramways Company Limited, who began their service in March 1883 with the opening of the section between the Market Place and Blackford Bridge and beyond.

The electric tram service came into operation in June 1903 with the Moorside to Jericho route and in the next four years trams ran from Bury to Heap Bridge, Limefield, Whitefield, Breightmet, Tottington and Radcliffe. The last sections to be completed were the lines to the new Inn, Walmersley and Smethurst Hall, Jericho, both in February 1915. The plate top right is of Tram No. 5, originally an open top car, later fitted with a roof.

In September 1925 a motor bus service was inaugurated between Bury and Walshaw, and the omnibus era had begun. The parts of the borough which were not served by trams were provided with a bus service, and there began a series of inter-running arrangements with the surrounding towns.

In March 1933, the Corporation decided to gradually abandon the tramway service, but the war intervened and it was not until February 1949 that the last tram ran on the Walmersley section and a chapter in Bury's history closed.

Bottom left: One of the steam trams on the Bury and Whitefield section. Advertisements for Cornalls the ironmongers of Haymarket Street, and Renshaws the boot seller of Princess Street were displayed on the steam engine.

Bottom right: Laying the section from Limefield to the New Inn, Walmersley, 1915.

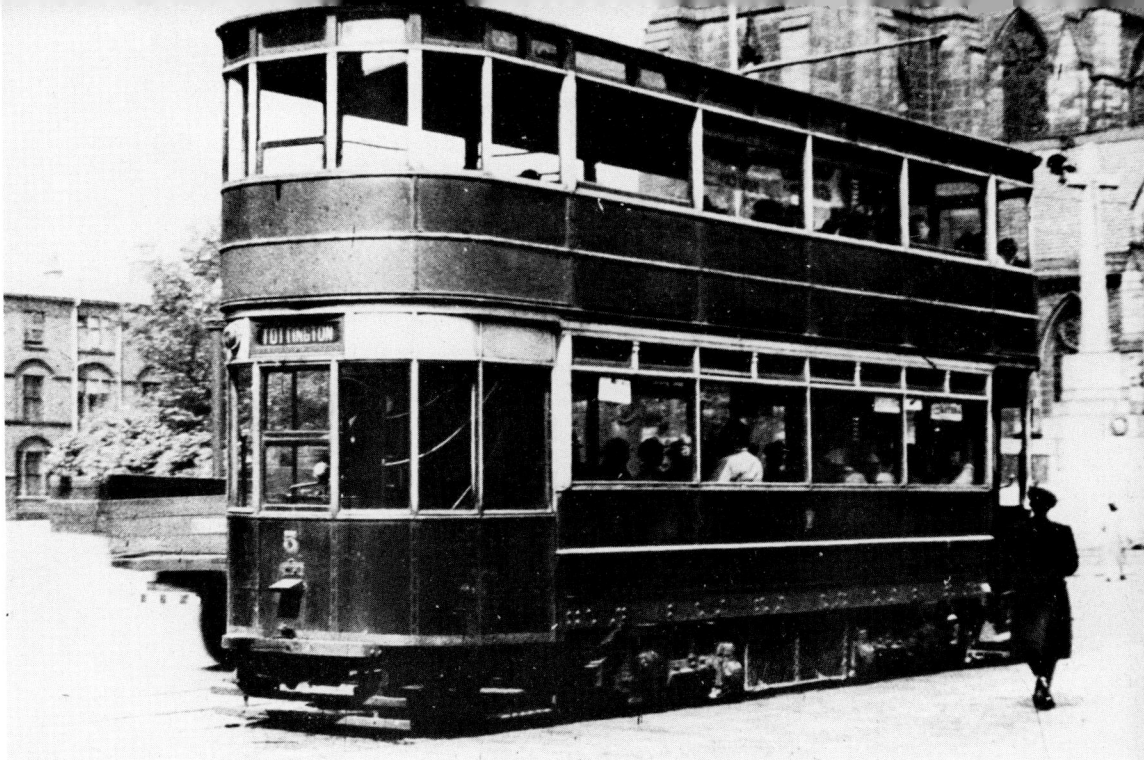

Left: Perhaps this photograph will nudge someone's memory as nobody seems to know what became of this fascinating piece of equipment—the Tramways Departments water cart. Manufactured by Mountain and Gibson of Harvey Street, Elton, the cart was used to flush out dust caught in the grooves of the track, and also to keep the tar cool on the sets. The tank was capable of holding 1800 gallons of water which was collected from a pipe connected to the reservoir at Clarence Park. The cart could be used for towing and it also possessed a grinding mechanism for smoothing out corrugations in the track.

Above: In the summer of 1922, Carrs of Knowsley Street proudly announced their seven day char-a-banc tour of Scotland for the princely sum of £10.10.0.!

We don't know the destination of this outing but for some reason all but two of the boys were seated in one 'chara' and all the girls in the other!

Originally a firm of cycle manufacturers and agents, Charles and William Carr established their business in Broad Street, where Barclays Bank now stands. The firm later moved to Fleet Street and then to Knowsley Street in 1911.

Left: The first time that a reigning monarch came to Bury was George V and Queen Mary's visit of July 1913.

The Royal party entered the Borough via Heap Bridge and the route along Rochdale Road was lined with thousands of school children vigorously waving Union Jacks. The junction of Clough Street and Rock Street was crowded with spectators who gave their Majesties an enthusiastic and noisy welcome. Almost every shop on Fleet Street was decorated and the Market Place was a blaze of colour.

The King and Queen (wearing a blue suit and white blouse) arrived at the Town Hall in Market Street and were welcomed by the Mayor, Alderman John Parks, who proudly boasted that Bury 'could claim to have the best back streets as well as the best front street in the country.'

Several local dignataries were presented to their Majesties and as the crowd cheered the King raised his hat in acknowledgement. The Royal party lunched in the Town Hall and outside the band of the 5th Battalion Lancashire Fusiliers (Territorials) played selections of operatic music.

The Royal party left Bury via Knowsley Street and Manchester Road and continued their tour of Lancashire towns.

A few days later Lord Derby received a letter from Lord Stamfordham, the King's private secretary saying that the King hoped that in future when his health is drunk, the wording of the toast be 'The King — the Duke of Lancaster.'

Right: 6th July 1921 and the Prince of Wales visit to Bury. It was a gloriously fine day (a later Royal visit was not to be favoured with such good weather) and the Prince arrived at the Derby Hall in an open-top Rolls-Royce car, accompanied by Lord Derby. The prince had specifically asked that there be no set decorative scheme by the local authority, but nevertheless public and commercial buildings were adorned with flags and garlands and the crowd provided a demonstration of their loyalty and affection. The Prince shook hands with a number of ex-servicemen, before dining at the Derby Hall.

An event not on the programme was the flight of an aeroplane over the town. To the delight of the young and the intense interest of the older inhabitants the plane 'looped-the-loop' several times.

COUNTY BOROUGH OF BURY.

LOCAL FOOD CONTROL COMMITTEE.

FOOD RATION CARD.

Holder's Name... *Albert Nelson*

Address ...... *6 South Bank Rd. Bury*

BUTTER AND/OR MARG.

Retailer's Regd. No. ....

Week ending	March.					April.				May.			
	X	X	16	23	30	6	13	20	27	4	11	18	25
	June.					July.				August.			
	1	8	15	22	29	6	13	20	27	3	10	17	24

TEA.

Retailer's Regd. No. ....

Week ending	March.					April.				May.			
	X	X	16	23	30	6	13	20	27	4	11	18	25
	June.					July.				August.			
	1	8	15	22	29	6	13	20	27	3	10	17	24

A.

Retailer's Regd. No. ....

Week ending	March.					April.				May.			
	X	X	16	23	30	6	13	20	27	4	11	18	25
	June.					July.				August.			
		8	15	22	29	6	13	20	27	3	10	17	24

B.

Retailer's Regd. No. ....

Week ending	March.					April.				May.			
	X	X	16	23	30	6	13	20	27	4	11	18	25
	June.					July.				August.			
	1	8	15	22	29	6	13	20	27	3	10	17	24

Far left: Gallipoli Day was commemorated on 28th April 1923 by a service at Bury Parish Church and a parade through the town centre. The service was attended by the Mayor, Councillor Redford, town council officials and troops from the Lancashire Fusiliers Wellington Barracks. Colonel Needham and the Mayor took the salute at the march past in the Market Place, and the parade was accompanied by the band of the 5th Battalion Lancashire Fusiliers.

Left: A food ration card issued by the Local Food Control Committee of the County Borough of Bury. Issued in 1915 to Albert Nelson of South Bank Road, the reverse of the card warns the user of a "£100 fine or six months imprisonment or both for the misuse of the card."

Top & bottom right:
In 1913, there were five veterinary surgeons in Bury, and Mr. W. E. S. Richmond had recently removed his practice from Silver Street to these premises at number 10 Knowsley Street—adjacent to Carrs Garage.

Top left: August 1st, 1908 and the opening of the Bury Children's Holiday Home at Birtle, by Alderman Butcher. A holiday home had previously been organised at Deeply Vale, but in 1908 Cuthbert Grundy of Blackpool presented this building to the committee. The home was run by volunteers and from Whitsuntide until the end of September the home could cater for twenty-five children a week. The home was intended for 8 to 14 year olds, irrespective of class or creed, but preference was given to the poorer children. Before the children were allowed into the home they had first to attend the public baths and were then taken by tram to Mawkin Lane, on the first step of their journey to enjoy the bracing air of Birtle. A former 'holidaymaker' at the home recalls the wholesome food, and the breakfasts of bread, treacle and cocoa!

Bottom left: An aerial view taken in the early 1930s on a busy market day. Kay Gardens, on the site of the old market were the gift of Henry Whitehead of Haslam Hey and were opened in 1908. The bus shelters were erected soon after this photograph was taken.

The buildings of Bury Co-operative Society figure prominently on this photograph—the Dairy on Georgiana Street (named after the wife of the Rev. Geoffrey Hornby) was opened in 1927 and Co-op Hall in Knowsley Street was built in 1869. Work on the Co-op Emporium did not begin until 1936.

The abattoirs were first used in 1902 and St. Maries School was built in 1909. The school was originally an all age school but later became a junior school when St. Gabriel's opened.

Right: Another aerial view taken at the same time. The corner of Union Square can just be seen in the bottom left corner, and the intense housing demolished to make way for the shopping precinct and Angouleme Way in the foreground.

St. Johns Church, built 1770, demolished 1967 can be seen on Stanley Street, and across the road the site now occupied by the Fire Station. New Road Congregational Chapel founded in 1792 by some of the members of Bank Street Presbyterian Chapel is shown and this building was erected in 1885.

Top left: The Royal Lancashire Show was held in Bury during August 1911 on a site near the Infirmary at Seedfield. The show was visited by Lord Derby, the president of the Society, and also by Councillor and Mrs. Bridge, the Mayor and Mayoress and Sir George Toulmin, the M.P. for Bury. Houses and shops on the route leading to the ground were decorated and special trains brought the spectators. On the first day rain fell in almost torential downpours, but some 12,000 people braved the elements to view sheep-dog trials, milking trials, horse parades and the other events which make up an agricultural show. One of the prizewinners at the show was the firm of H. Halstead, provision merchants of the Market Hall, who won first and second prizes for Lancashire cheese. On the Sunday, a special service was held, and it was conducted by the Rev. R. P. Hudson, the vicar of St. Johns, in whose parish the showground was situated. The forerunner of the Royal Lancashire Show, the Royal Manchester, Liverpool and District Show had previously visited Bury in 1891 and the showground was then situated at Limefield, although in a different position. The 'Bury Guardian' of 5th August 1911 reported that ''Bury has not been itself this week. There has been introduced into it a cosmopolitanism which is as exceptional as it is welcome. The streets have been busier, strange faces have been seen, fresh tongues have been heard, and there has been a ceaseless activity infusing a busy aspect which it would be well for the borough were it more frequent''.

Bottom left: Very conveniently for us, the newsboy's placard announcing the death of M'Kinley, the American president, pinpoints the date as September 1901.

Tithebarn Street, viewed here from Parsons Lane, was of course named after the tithebarn which still stands and is now a second-hand shop.

Right: The elegant facade of the Derby Hotel was a well beloved landmark for many Buryites. It opened for business in February 1850 and together with the Derby Hall and the Athenaeum it formed one of the town's best known architectural features. The hotel was designed by Sydney Smirke, a distinguished architect of the time and was part of a commercial inn and town hall building commissioned by the Earl of Derby. More than

once Royalty were entertained at the hotel, and at one time there was stabling for fifteen horses.

By 1964 the hotel had ceased to be a viable proposition and the brewery sold the building to a development company. After many months of heart searching by councillors and officials the decision to demolish the hotel was made and in 1965 the deed was done.

A macabre, 'double suicide' took place at the Derby Hotel in 1899. Mr. John Knight, a Belgian and his ladyfriend Mlle. L. F. Rousseau arrived at the Derby Hotel and signed the register, using, as it was later proved, false names. Mr. Knight enquired if there was a chemist's shop nearby, and the couple duly visited the shop at 14 Bolton Street, but failing to get what they wanted, they tried Clifton's in Fleet Street. On returning to the hotel, the couple entered their bedroom and asked not to be disturbed.

By noon the following day the manager became anxious about the couple's non-appearance, and when he discovered that the bedroom door was locked from the inside, a ladder was put up to the bedroom window. The couple were found dead in bed, clasped in each others arms. A letter was found, addressed to the coroner, with money to cover the funeral expenses. The letter indicated that the couple had used false names for some time and that attempts to identify them would be fruitless. Marks of identification had been removed from the couple's belongings, but eventually the man's name was found to have been written inside his trousers by his tailor in London.

Mlle. Rousseau was buried in Bury Cemetery, whilst Mr. Knight's body was shipped to the Netherlands. Mr. Knight was a member of an aristocratic family and was a partner in a wealthy firm of insurance brokers. He was also Consul to Turkey and Belgium.

Why Bury was chosen for the suicide was never established.

Left: Bury Infirmary as this building was known opened in 1882. As early as 1829, a Dispensary was founded in Bolton Street and by contributing to a fund, Bury people could obtain drugs and treatment. In 1841 the Dispensary moved into the building on the corner of Moss Street and Knowsley Street—now occupied by the Athenaeum. Pressures on the service increased and in 1873 Lord Derby gave five acres of land at Littlewood Cross for the express purpose of building an infirmary. With a legacy from Thomas Norris, a former Bury man, and £10,000 from Thomas Wrigley's estate, an appeal was launched and the prospect of a real infirmary came nearer.

The children's ward was opened by Lord Derby in July 1923 and it was intended as a war memorial to the men of Bury who fell in the Great War. Along with many other public buildings, it was built by Messrs. Thompson & Brierley of Bury.

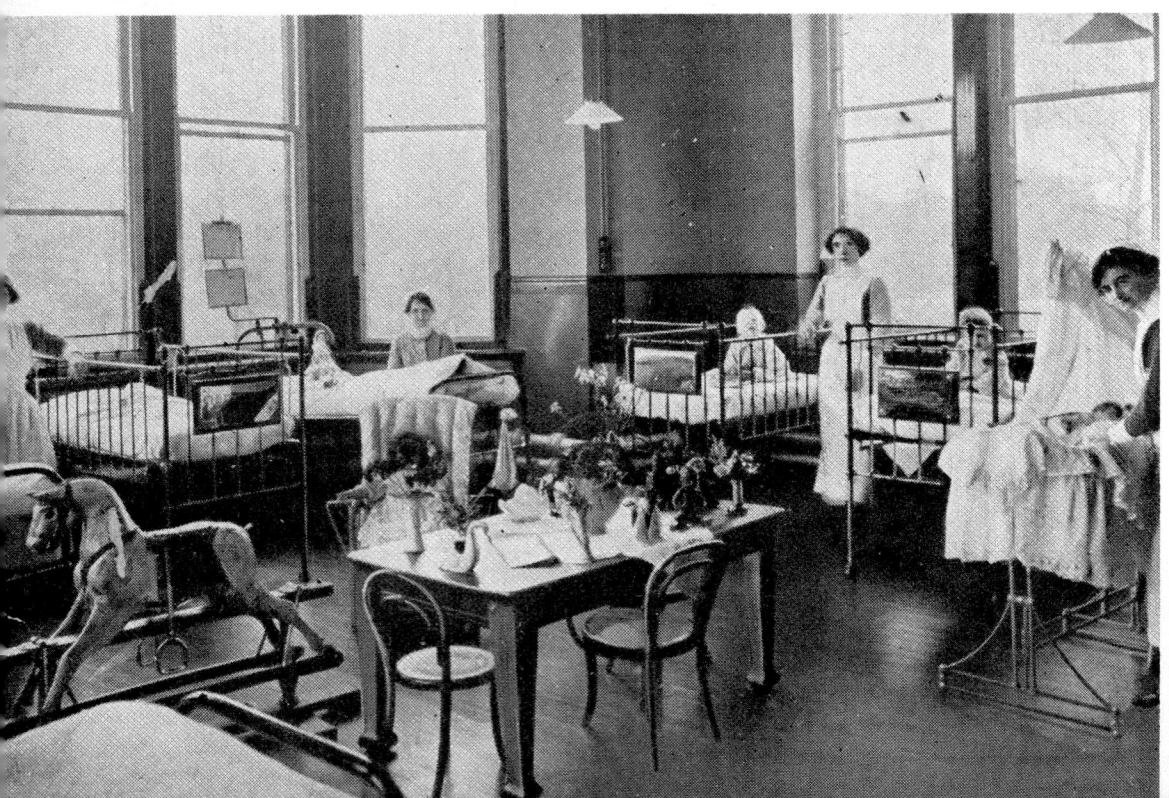

Right: Another event which could be commemorated in 1976 is the 75th Anniversary of the Art Gallery and Library.

In the 1890s, whilst many Lancashire towns were busy adopting the Public Libraries Acts, Bury people on the whole, were not too enthusiastic, as both the Co-op and the Athenaeum already provided reading rooms and lending library facilities. The gift to the town of the fine Wrigley collection of paintings and drawings prompted the Corporation into action, and in 1897 it was announced that Mrs. Davies of Rhiwlas intended to found and endow a reading room for women. An Art Gallery Committee of the Town Council was formed and they purchased the land on the corner of Moss Lane, where Broom Hall, Colonel Hutchinson's house had stood.

Tenders for the design of the building were invited and the Art Gallery and Library, built by Messrs, Thompson and Brierley, was officially opened on 9th October, 1901, by Lord Derby.

Left: Now occupied by the Libraries Department, the Textile Hall was built to house the offices of the various textile unions in the town. Previously the unions had offices in different parts of the town, but the noise made by the worker's clogs as they visited their unions, made it difficult for the unions to find adequate premises.

The hall was built on land leased by Lord Derby to the Hutchinson family, and part of Broom Hall, the Hutchinson's family home can be seen on the left of the photograph.

Lady Emilia Dilke, a philanthropist and campaigner for the rights of cotton operatives, opened the hall on 5th May 1894, and a procession through the town centre composed of eighteen bands and vehicles and waggonettes enlivened the proceedings. The stone carvings on the Yorkshire stone frontage depict different branches of the textile industry, and the observant will notice that apart from the removal of the tower, railings and windows, the hall has changed very little, externally, in the eighty years of its existence.

Right: Whilst some parts of Bury have remained virtually unaltered, other parts have changed so much that they are beyond recognition. Bolton Street is one such area and this view, taken about 1900 is of the area now covered by the roundabout at Castlecroft.

Top left: Stanley Street again, this time the building on the site of the old Fire Station, which was demolished in 1967. The present Fire Station adjoins the site of the previous building—parts of which were erected in 1925. The new building also extends over what was Horrocks Fold, shown bottom left.

In the Bury Vestry Minutes for 1793 there is noted the purchase of two fire engines made by a Mr. Winlaw of London. The Bury Improvement Act of 1846 allowed the employment of firemen and superintendents, and the purchase of fire engines and fire fighting equipment. Bury's first steam engine, bought in March 1875 was made by Shand, Mason & Co., and it was drawn by two horses—four horses were necessary if the engine was required at an out of town fire.

The annual report of the Fire Brigade for 1910 in its list of equipment records for the first time 'a petrol motor machine'. In 1913 a Leyland Motors fire engine was acquired which was capable of delivering over 500 gallons of water a minute.

The fire station opened in 1925 by Alderman Sanderson could accommondate four engines and one ambulance, plus housing for the Superintendent and a recreation room for the firemen. The cost was £7,000, considerably less than the original estimate.

The Library's oldest photograph! Taken in 1852 when photography was still young, the photograph shows the horse bus service which ran between Bury and Whitefield.

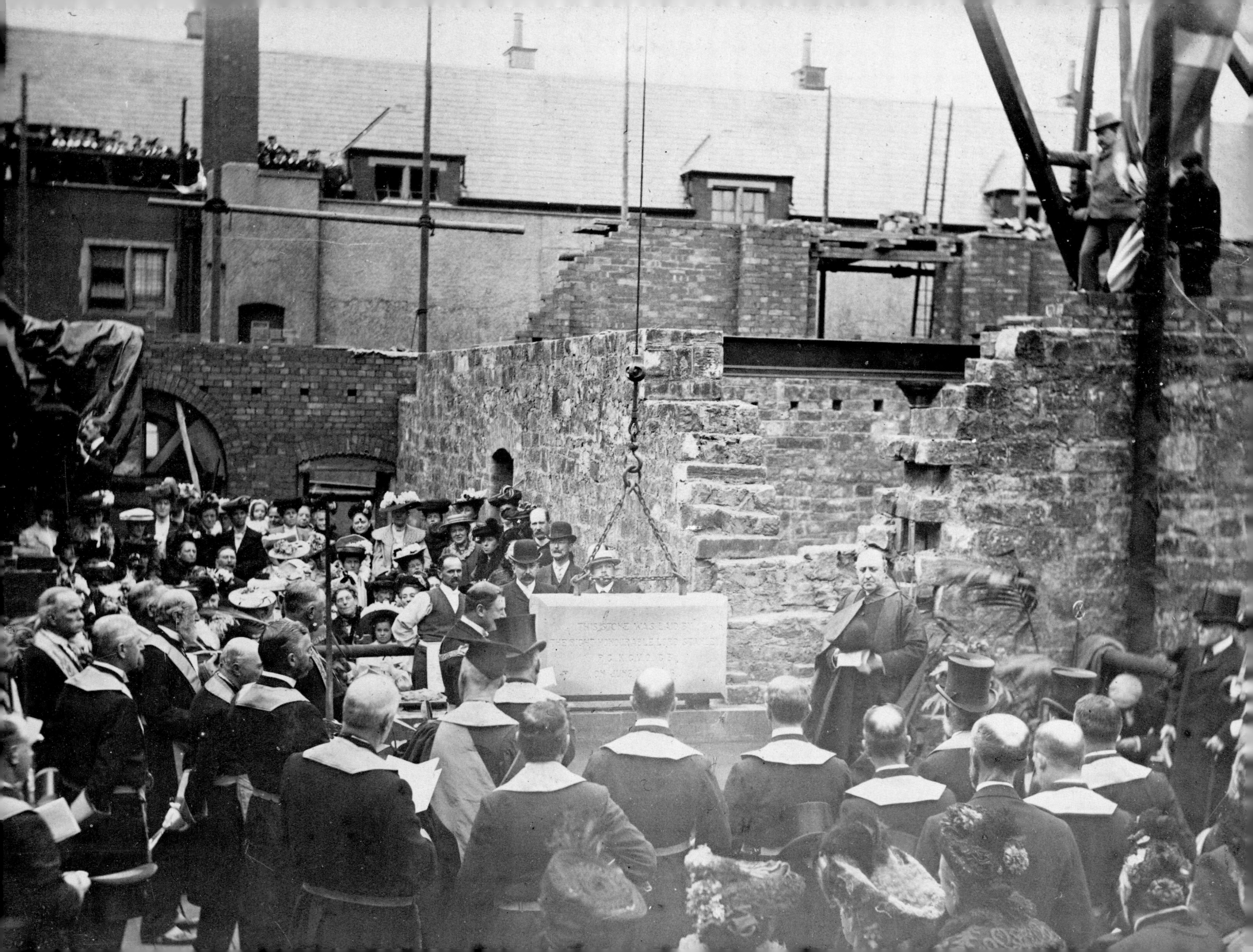

The plate on the facing page shows the Bury Grammar School for Boys and Lord Stanley laying the foundation stone of the new Assembly Hall on 25th June, 1906.

It was only on special occasions that a full Masonic ceremony was witnessed and the striking appearance of the Brethren in their full dress Grand Lodge clothing made it a memorable experience.

The cost of the hall was met by Mr. H. Whitehead, a Past Provincial Grand Warden and Lord Stanley was Grand Master. The stone was laid, Lord Stanley pronounced it to be "plumb, level and square" and declared that the craftsmen had worked well. Corn, to typify plenty, wine to typify joy and oil, the emblem of peace were poured over the stone. The hall, which cost over £4,000 was opened by Lady Stanley in March 1907.

Right: Probably most people are familiar with the story as to how the 'Two Tubs' got its name, but for those who don't know, the story dates back to the 1830s when the 'Toasted Cheese Club' met regularly at the inn, then known as the 'Globe Inn'. One evening a member of the club noticed that a new sign was being erected at the 'Old White Bear'. So as not to be outdone, the club members and the landlord decided that the 'Globe' needed a new sign. A man named Shaw had the bright idea of fixing the two halves of a barrel over the door and so the following day the barrel was placed in position and painted. The two halves were meant to represent the two hemispheres, the staves the longitude and the bands the latitude. The inn soon came to be called the 'Two Tubs' but even today, its correct designation is still 'The Globe'.

Top right: The 'Two Tubs', The Wylde about 1890.

Bottom right: The Wylde and the Market Place in 1933. In 1920 the South African War Memorial was moved from the Market Place to its present site in the Whitehead Gardens.

Left: Another pub with an unusual name, this time the 'Hark to Towler' at Limefield. According to the popular story, Towler was a beagle dog with a remarkable bark. Indeed, a dog named Towler did run with the Holcombe Hunt and a hunting song in his honour was composed by John Jackson, the Master of the Hunt.

Horse buses were a popular feature of the day and the one shown is the service which ran between Edenfield and Bury.

The 'Old Duke Inn, Brandlesholme Road was originally a coaching inn used by travellers on route to Blackburn. It is believed to have been named after the Duke of Wellington, who died in 1852, and it was well-known for its welcoming fires burning in the grate and for its beautiful oak beams, John Elford, was the landlord from about 1894 to 1899, and the ale was supplied by Chadwick's Walmersley Brewery.

Chadwick's Brewery is first mentioned in the 1841 directory as James and Robert Chadwick, ale and porter brewers, and in 1851 they are described as being at Pigslee. The former brewery still stands—the premises now being occupied by Spurrier Glazebrook. Chadwicks took over one or two smaller breweries in the 1890s and in 1933 they themselves were taken over by Wilsons of Manchester.

A number of town centre inns had their own concert halls and the 'Dog Inn' situated off Crompton Street was one of them. The inn stood in what was formerly known by the unsavoury name of 'Gutter Ends' and was demolished in July 1926. In 1908 the local magistrates had refused to renew the inn's license and for many years the inn was used for storage until its demolition. The site was acquired by the Post Office for the building of their garages and nowadays it is almost impossible to trace the site of the inn. The building behind the inn is Union Street Methodist Church and possibly at one time the inn gave access to the bowling green which occupied the site where the chapel was built in 1816.

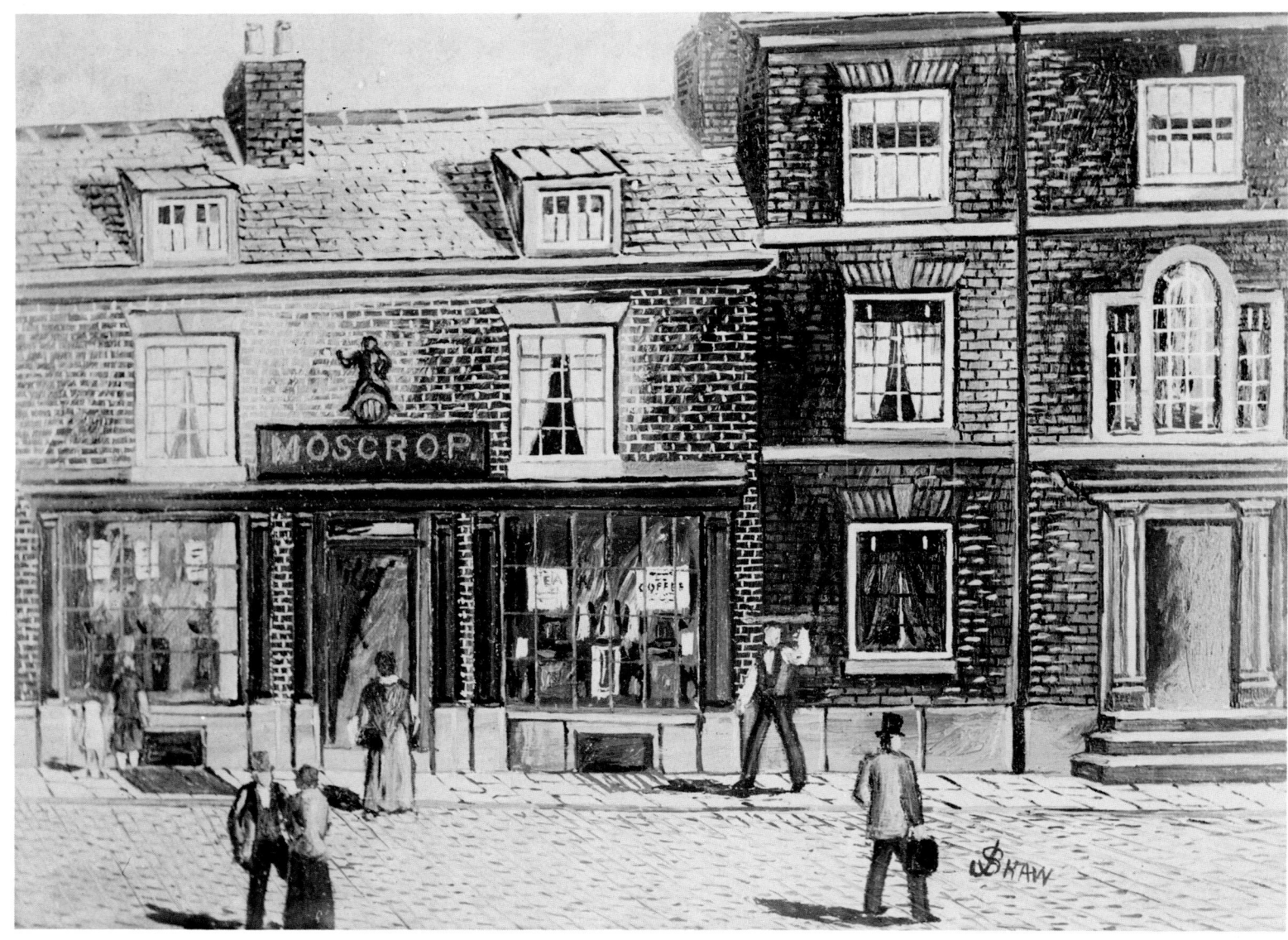

Well-known for his paintings and drawings of Bury was the artist of this picture, James 'Clock' Shaw, born in Bury in 1836. James acquired his rather unusual nickname as a result of his father having a clock in front of his house in The Wylde. James' father had been a member of the Vestry—the body of people who ran the town prior to the appointment of the Improvement Commissioners—and for his services he and two other worthies were presented with a public clock. Eventually the clock came into the possession of James Shaw and as his father's premises were to be demolished James gave the clock to the Local Volunteer Corps, and the clock was placed in the tower of the Drill Hall.

James died in September 1915, by which time he had sketched and painted many views of Victorian and Edwardian Bury. Fortunately many of his pictures have survived and are preserved in the Art Gallery.